GARDEN WEIGHTS: AN ORIGINAL STAGE PLAY

By

Andrew Busingye

KHAMEL
PUBLISHING

This book has been published in print, e-format and sold on Amazon.com by KHAMEL Publishing
www.khamelpublishing.com

ISBN: 978-9970-9453-7-5
© Andrew Busingye 2016
Second edition

ABOUT THE AUTHOR

The playwright Andrew Busingye was born in South Western Uganda, studied and taught Literature in English at Secondary School level before undertaking Business and Entrepreneurship studies at Makerere University, Uganda.

He may be reached at this address:

Andrew Busingye
P.O. Box 30183
Kampala, Uganda
Tel: +256 774 442830
E-mail: **abusingye48@gmail.com**

ACKNOWLEDGEMENTS

Special thanks go out to my parents who gave me the basics of life, the school and teachers who worked hard to bring out the best in me and the resourceful support of KHAMEL Publishing and Razor Agency Ltd to make this publication a reality.

- Andrew.

TABLE OF CONTENTS

Garden Weights: An Original Stage Play..................1

About the Author..4

Acknowledgements..5

Garden Weights: An Original Stage Play..................8

Cast of Characters...9

ACT I

    Scene 1...11

    Scene 2...16

    Scene 3...32

    Scene 4...37

ACT II

    Scene 1...47

    Scene 2...62

    Scene 3...74

ACT III

    Scene 1...82

    Final Scene...96

GARDEN WEIGHTS: AN ORIGINAL STAGE PLAY

By

Andrew Busingye

CAST OF CHARACTERS

KONDO   President of Munga
                           Farmers Union

ZAMWE   Prominent lawyer and

                           speaker of Munga Farmers
                           Union

BANDA   Munga Union treasurer

SHAPA   Union secretary

MURA   Executive farmers'

                           Representative

KANGINE   Executive farmers'

                           Representative

WENDA	Journalist
OTHERS	1st Farmer
	2nd Farmer
	3rd Farmer

ACT I

SCENE 1

(Birds hum away in mid-morning hours. On gentle sloping land, a man is seen digging under the blistering sun. He stops the work, stretches and yawns. He puts the hoe on his shoulder and slowly walks away.)

MURA: *(He dusts soil off his trousers as he sings softly.)*

ENOUGH OF THE DAY'S WORK.

COME ON MY SON.

MOTHER HAS THE DISH READY.

TAKE IT SON AND WAIT FOR THE RAINS.

TO BLESS YOUR WORKS. *(His voice gets louder.)* MAKE IT TO THE WELL SON!

THE COWS WAIT FOR YOU...

(Someone coughing interrupts the singing and Mura turns.)

KONDO: (*Enters from the side, dressed in dark sunglasses and holding a leather bag.*) Hey Bwana, when did you become a musician?

MURA: Cowboy habits die-hard. We recall the old warrior's tunes.

KONDO: That's it! Thanks for the farm work. I have been moving from house to house searching for my people. (*Wipes sweat off his face.*) A friend in London called yesterday to inform me of the heavy rains those ends. (*The pair walks slowly along the path.*) It is going to be five weeks of non-stop mist and rainy days!

MURA: Climate differs from region to region. For the last six years, we have been having calculating sunny and rainy intervals, with the latter gracing us at night mostly. Now that it has rained once, we cannot easily predict the next showers.

KONDO: Those are old outdated statistics, my friend. We live in modern, more scientific times. It was even raining in China according to last night's news on television. Better style up, old man.

MURA: *(Visibly irritated.)* This is Africa. What have London or China got to do with our own natural climate? Wake up from‐

(Kondo quickly cuts in.)

KONDO: Hey, I've brought you samples of the new improved fertilizer to improve on yields this season. It has been recommended by leading professors. *(Removes paper packet from his bag.)* You can have a look.

MURA: This is like that damned stuff that killed our maize gardens a few years back. We are better off without it.

KONDO: You never followed the application instructions. Besides, this is a new and improved version.

MURA: That is what you always say. Tell me, did the whole village get the application procedures wrong?

KONDO: The acidic rains and heavy drought also had a role to play in the damages.

MURA: Then why risk it again with your costly foreign substances when the farmyard manure lies idle in our kraals?

(*Hands him back the samples.*)

KONDO: At times we need both in case-

MURA: (*Rushing offstage.*) Not me at least. My cows need a drink, see you later.

(Kondo is left alone onstage as he wipes sweat off his face.)

KONDO: That man has always been a thorn in my side, constantly thwarting all my strategic plans by charming away my would-be followers. I need another term in the Farmers Union presidential seat and the Tender Board chairmanship. I bring them modern fertilizers but the peasants seem to love living in the past. This is a new era, a new brand, and a change for the better.

(End of Scene I of Act I. Curtains are drawn.)

SCENE 2

(In a fairly decorated hall, farmers are gathered in large numbers for the monthly union briefing. Some are seen murmuring, chatting and laughing while others concentrate on paper work. A few attendants move up and down. A drum sound is heard.)

KONDO: *(From a seat at the high table.)* Ladies and gentlemen! Today, I temporarily assume the speaker's role since our honorable speaker hasn't returned from her holiday.

Still, I will have to make my mandatory president's speech and comments on the planned elections, as well as the way forward as indicated on the agenda.

1ST FARMER: Members, is it in order for one to become a moderator of oneself? We cannot have a presidential-speaker- participant, not now.

BANDA: Why not? He is capable, he has done it before and after all, the constitution does not mention of such prohibition.

SHAPA: Take it easy guys. We would have had the deputy speaker in charge, but she too is unable to come as she is busy with an upcountry crusade. She sent it in her apologies, so let us adapt to the situation.

KONDO: I hope the issue is solved. Can we proceed with the issues on the agenda?

2ND FARMER: I have not got a copy of the current financial statement plus the second refreshment drink served.

(*Laughter from other farmers.*)

KONDO: Sorry for the shortage in copies. I'm told it is due to a machine breakdown. Maybe you can get the second drink as compensation for that! (*More laughter.*) The constitution is yet to provide for such trivia!

MURA: On a more serious note, can I know why there is such a dramatic fall in the market produce revenue, as indicated in the financial paper?

KONDO: It was even said on radio that there is a fall in world markets due to the increase in oil prices and the wave of terrorist attacks in Europe. Yet much of our produce, all the way here in Africa suffered as a result of negative market trends.

MURA: The previous markets promotions circular indicated the availability of similar demands in Asia and Southern Africa, so why not channel the produce there if Europe has proved unfavorable?

KONDO: That would call for extra costs because transporting to those other markets is not cost effective, as Europe is the trend setter in pricing.

(Low jeers.)

1ST FARMER: *(Standing.)* Why did the treasury authorize payment of six million shillings from the union's coffers to pay lawyers in a private case? The constitution clearly spells out that money should be spent on activities concerning the union or those in which it has interests.

(Heads turn.)

BANDA: The money in question was paid out to lawyers acting on our President's behalf. Since Mr. Kondo is our democratically elected leader, he represents Munga Farmers Union, thus the legal obligation to save our image in every possible way.

(Loud protests.)

MURA: Impossible! The court case was purely a personal matter. One's individual dishonesty and lack of integrity need not be amended by the union. If this is allowed to pass, we might soon have bedroom matters in the official records.

2ND FARMER: The money must be refunded and an apology made for such a sin committed without even consulting us members who provide the funds.

(*Loud applause.*)

1ST FARMER: (*Furious.*) My earlier concern of a mediator becoming part of the audience is now quelled. The current speaker is presiding over a system that is about to crucify him.

(*Cheers.*)

BANDA: Do not worry, it was never a serious case, it never went far, in fact it only ended as mere allegations of corruption. The judge cleared us- (*Boos from the farmers.*) Money well spent.

SHAPA: I'm of the view that we immediately select a stand-in mediator from the audience, so as to allow Mr. Kondo to take part in the proceedings without clash of interest.

(*More boos.*)

KONDO: No need for all that process. I can deliver and respond to every query without resigning temporarily. I have done it before-

(*Louder boos.*)

MURA: This cannot go on like this! Daylight robbery is disrespect of the highest order. I call for a boycott now until a better and more just line of order, presided over by our democratically elected speaker, is put in place.

(Mura picks his file and moves out as others follow him to the exit. Banda and a few heads try to persuade the volatile members to stay but to no avail. They too exit but Kondo, Shapa and a journalist remain in the hall. Shapa and Kondo remain on the high table as Wenda joins them from behind.)

SHAPA: Mr. Chairman, I missed a part of your opening speech in the minutes. May you repeat the bit of...

(Putting papers together...)

KONDO: *(Furious.)* Where were you? I'm tired of your excuses after every meeting. You even disgraced me by calling for my temporary resignation! Better resign your position too before-

SHAPA: *(Annoyed.)* Sir, I was just trying to cool the situation to suit your interest and that of the executive.

KONDO: Shut up! (*Bangs table with fist.*) Hey journeyman! (*Turns to Wenda.*) Hope you know what to report on and what to leave out. The other time I paid you double to have my photo on the front page but I never saw it there.

WENDA: Sir, the editor is the one to blame. I played my part and gave him the parcel and he promised to do the needful.

(*Meanwhile, Shapa has his head downcast.*)

KONDO: Now, promise that it will make the front page and have a big headline reading something like "Kondo steers Munga Forward", with details of my plans for the globalization of agriculture.

WENDA: The photo can possibly make it but a big headline has to wait for Thursday's business magazine.

KONDO: What makes it impossible for the headline? I'm tripling the usual tea to the editor.

(*He reaches for his wallet.*)

WENDA: (*In a pleading tone.*) My Boss, the paper has clearly defined rules we cannot ignore. Big business stories like yours are for Thursday's business magazine.

SHAPA: (*Drawing closer.*) Mr. Chairman, I need to rush home and attend to my sick wife. So you may pay me the day's allowance now.

KONDO: (*Angry.*) Is that why you dozed and missed my opening remarks? Don't carry family matters into the union. Give a copy of our yearly plan to Mr. Wenda for publication too.

SHAPA: I left the file at home since it was not on the agenda. Maybe he can come along to pick it.

WENDA: My Boss that will be too much stuff to run in a single story. Maybe in a fortnight...

KONDO: (*Surprised.*) Eeh! You people lack vision and sharp minds in the games of manipulation and leadership. We've got to get things moving, because next week we enter a new phase, money does.

SHAPA: If so, may I get the day's allowance paid? Because tomorrow never comes.

KONDO: Wait till I return from the bank. Your share is now attached to Wenda's tea in the interest of our union.

SHAPA: My wife needs medication badly and the doctor has not been paid for the first dose.

WENDA: I should also have tea for the business editor since he is the final person to handle our stories for publication.

KONDO: (*Enraged.*) You people! Cheats! Why demand a lot in times of disaster? You never sweat for this. Shapa missed the all-important opening remarks. Wenda cost me public support for having my photo in the middle pages, the last time.

SHAPA: Cool down sir. For the sake of my family and my wife's life, I beg to have it now.

WENDA: My boss, we follow certain steps and rules and mind you, I'm only a junior reporter.

KONDO: Parasites! (*Irritated.*) Don't waste my time. I'm capable of sorting out all this on my own! My fresh graduate daughter will do better!

(Picks up his files and moves towards exit.)

SHAPA: Are you trying to say I'm fired? By you alone? *(Laughs.)* I was elected by a majority vote, mind you.

KONDO: *(Stops and looks back.)* You forget that the rules booklet empowers a chairman to discipline any incompetent member. As for you Wenda, I'm going to see the editor myself. Direct. No more cheating brokers.

(He storms out in quick steps and exits. Left on stage, Wenda and Shapa stand confused, one folds his arms and the other scratches his head as the sound of a flute plays in the background.)

WENDA: Are we paying the price of loyalty?

SHAPA: I could see it raining on me from the day he suggested having my field report edited by his *fresh graduate* daughter.

WENDA: Has he only accused you of inefficiency in recording minutes, or do you have other sins?

SHAPA: *(Shakes his head.)* Just lame and false excuses to have me on the ropes. I had to sacrifice a lot and risk the life of my wife to attend the bloody meeting. If only he could recall my valuable contributions in his past court cases.

WENDA: Ya, I recall those moments. *(Laughs heartily.)* He survived narrowly. The envelopes were all over the place. I even got one to have press reports neutralized.

SHAPA: He is good at that. Two days prior to the commencement of the court hearings, he camped at my house for twenty-four hours with two lawyers. They had many records and minutes manipulated and some created.

WENDA: What of the members' signatures? Were they tricked into signing again?

SHAPA: That is the easiest underground booming business. Some crooks earn millions by specializing in signature recreation. In fact these crooks collaborate well with lawyers in town.

WENDA: Your boss now seems to face less fire from the ordinary farmers. He may easily earn another term.

SHAPA: You see, the few members who raise eyebrows are easily greased with *tea*. Most are illiterate peasants who are put off by mega promises and bureaucracy.

WENDA: How come the likes of you elite animals keep silent amidst this rot? Wait, you are probably part of the bigger eating circuit.

(*He laughs.*)

SHAPA: Man, at times you are made to sacrifice professional ethics at the altar of family bread.

WENDA: Now, the hunter is hunted. They say, practice what you preach! *(Laughs louder.)* Got to look for ways to revenge man!

SHAPA: We are in the same boat, man. The aid is off and you are now left on that meager per work allowance, so no more wine. *(He laughs.)* See you at the club tonight. Let me at least save my wife's life.

(Wenda is left alone on stage, and turns to audience as a low guitar plays in the background. The lights change.)

WENDA: Members, did we realize how Miss Gardens of planet earth faced the wrath of visionary Mr. Cultivator? Originally, little Gardens was a fertile virgin before Mr. Cultivator knelt and proposed to her, to at least mature his child in the interest of his professional life. The next season, Honorable Cultivator returns to her, this time asking for a bigger child from little Garden. In tears, poor Garden agrees but reminds Honorable Cultivator of the need to apply manure in her, so as to realize the need for bigger children.

The advice is ignored or dismissed altogether. Halfway into the pregnancy, there are signs of poor child growth in the womb. Instead of focusing on saving the sick unborn child, the Honorable is now scolding poor Ms Garden and threatening her. Who is to blame, really?

(Taking a seat, and birds singing in the background, Wenda is seen making gestures to an imaginary tree for an answer.)

Yes. Old Weaver Bird witnessed the whole scenario from the comfort of the tree top and says "Poor Ms Garden should have first weighed the risks and benefits of flirting with big cultivators."*(Pauses a bit before pointing up again.)* Mrs. Weaver Bird in the branch below asks, "How could she have resisted such a sweet-talking, smart and rich guy with magic words accompanying the nice smooth touches?" What is your take?

(Bends towards audience with hand on ear in anticipation of a reply.)

(End of Scene 2 of Act I.)

SCENE 3

(Mura with a hoe on the shoulder and panga in the other hand, meets Shapa who is from hospital with medicine for his wife.)

MURA: How is 'mamma' baby, big boy? Sorry for the axe man, Wenda told me of it man! (*Laughs a bit.*)

SHAPA: Firstly, the 'mamma' is fast improving and secondly, the axe is just imaginary because no man can wield it alone on a democratically elected tree.

MURA: The special man can take cover in the constitution to deal with you bad members.

SHAPA: Better get prepared too, I heard him complain of you campaigning against his big fertilizer project. Watch out for the axe, man!

(He smiles.)

MURA: That man thinks he can drive us into his personal whims and wishes any time. Has he forgotten the hell he put us through with the junk fertilizers? *(Spits.)* He was lucky to survive that court trial.

SHAPA: Had it not been for my corporation, the big man would now be in the comfort of a labour camp rubbing shoulders with convicted drug dealers and rapists.

MURA: I heard you talk of how you hid the forgery files and presented cleansed ones before court. You of course, made a fortune out of that hell, man!

(Pats Shapa on shoulder.)

SHAPA: *(Smiles a little.)* It was worth it, I even had to fabricate minutes of the infamous tender Board meeting held in his house.

MURA: Why did you, top men, exclude me from that golden tender team when by virtue of my position I'm supposed to be a part?

SHAPA: On the grounds of being suspected of harmful views to the union's visionary grand plan. (*Laughs a bit.*)

MURA: A vision of selfish, scandalous and thieving ideals pushed by sectarian and shallow minded individuals! (*Spits.*) Thank God I was never there to face probe teams and court trials.

(*Raises arms in disgust.*)

SHAPA: Truthfully, you have been deemed as a stumbling block on the big man's way to regain majority support of the common man.

MURA: Now, I think you are an additional stumbling block young man.

(Pats him on shoulder.)

SHAPA: In fact, the blocks are now three because Wenda too got caught in it and he vows to hit the big man where it hurts the most. *(He suddenly remembers.)* My dear wife's health is calling.

(He moves off stage in big strides.)

MURA: *(He shouts after him.)* You learnt lessons of a goat offering to escape a lion into the wilderness!

(Shapa exits with forced laughter. Silence ensues. Mura takes two calculated steps, stops, and then faces audience.)

MURA: The very day this young man inherited his father's position in the union, I warned him against being *used*. His father was a focused and principled person who struggled for the union's registration. He formed the historical band and had made a fortune out of farming, but the young man seems to be rapidly working against it.

Upon great Shapa's death, we spent a whole six days before the actual burial doing bull roasting on a daily basis. He had inspired many of us into what we are today. He laid the foundation with unbound determination.

Can the young, educated, modern and youthful generation spare the *green* legacy? I can hear the old man turning in his grave.

(Raises arms heavenward with his back to the audience, and a slow guitar tune plays in background.)

(End of Scene 3 of Act I. Curtains are drawn.)

SCENE 4

(Inside a modern living room, two men sit facing each other. Flasks, cups, wine bottles and glasses lie on a table in the middle. Newspapers are their point of concentration.)

BANDA: *(Sighing heavily.)* I can't believe this! Disaster and catastrophe! How could the editor allow *this* after that fat cheque we signed him a few days back? Maybe he ate it alone?

KONDO: He could not have given the other relevant heads their share. A big setback. Now all is lost.

(Drops paper on the floor in frustration and anger.)

BANDA: *(Holding paper more closely.)* Look! Here the fool asserts that the treasurer and president built a multi-million dollar hotel by the riverbank using the stolen funds. Son of a bitch!

(Drops paper and falls back into couch.)

KONDO: The headline itself is too traumatizing. The radio bastards were making fun of it before you came in. I accidentally knocked my hi-tech radio off the shelf in a bid to switch off the mockery.

BANDA: Couldn't that stubborn head, Shapa, have had a hand in this? How could the anonymous reporter get access to the copy of the cheque we paid to the site engineer?

KONDO: That is why I wanted him replaced with my daughter in the crucial record-keeping field.

BANDA: Anyway, did you pay him his allowance arrears the other day? I told him to get his share from you.

KONDO: The fool was supposed to seek me out after I had gone to the bank but *it* never showed up.

BANDA: I'm told you had verbally suspended him. You should have first cleared him. What if he legally sues you? In fact, that may be the point behind this part *(points to newspaper)* talking of misappropriation of members' allowances.

KONDO: *(Picking up paper.)* I feel terribly weak. How could this escape the editor's eye after we fed him enough?

BANDA: Maybe we forgot to warn him against printing the history. We never mentioned anything like leaving the crude past out.

KONDO: Common sense is all it takes to figure that out.

BANDA: Remember, their sales go soaring after creating such a saga.

By the way, there is an independent business editor whom we never saw personally. Could be the cause.

KONDO: Now, they want us to plead again through our pockets, then all they do is inject more poison from nowhere. I'm tired of this thieving cycle! Bastards! Only thinking of coins at the expense of one's public image.

(Hits hand on the table and falls back onto couch.)

BANDA: Apparently we have no other channel. We have got to bend low for them.

KONDO: They must stop this silly habit. I'm in no mood to compromise my grand plans for the sake of little fellows.

BANDA: Don't you think we need to call a crisis meeting? *(He pauses.)* No- let's call it an extraordinary meeting. We then put on stake higher sitting allowances for a massive turn up.

(Downs his glass.)

KONDO: I too thought of that but we need to be strategic and avoid the previous mess. The likes of Shapa and company need to be formally sidelined. A motion to unseat Shapa and Mura has to be moved.

BANDA: Any possible replacements on hand?

KONDO: My daughter is already warming up for the secretary's seat, so I'll give you a chance to choose Mura's successor.

BANDA: But first, we need the speaker back as fast as possible, lest we witness another boycott. With her back, we have no excuse from the elite bastards.

KONDO: That damned bitch! Having fun on sunny beaches as we toil and flex these ends!

(Downs his glass.)

BANDA: The rules booklet commands moving of a motion through the speaker, who in turn throws it to the house for debate.

KONDO: We therefore need majority backing from the local farmers. There we shall counter hothead Mura in his own backyard.

BANDA: The Wenda - Shapa duo is another menace.

KONDO: Strictly no journalist in this meeting then. Shapa is still a novice unless guided around by a few admirers of his late father's legacy.

(A servant enters with more wine bottles to replace the empty ones.)

BANDA: The immediate hurdle is now to rush back that fat lady speaker for duty as soon as possible. Should we send her a double air ticket, a few millions and perhaps promise another all expenses paid holiday?

KONDO: Ya, that sounds like a nice deal worth the importance of the meeting. She should not hesitate. Better get started on that now. I'm going to call that Iscariot editor a bit later.

(He rises and stretches. Drum beat sounds are heard.)

BANDA: *(Gets up too.)* Send your daughter to work on the air tickets stuff as I go to the bank for the money transfer deal. No time to waste.

(He rushes across the room to the door and exits.)

KONDO: *(Trots across the room, looks up and down, drinks from his whisky bottle, then faces audience.)* My grandpa used to consult old Shala in such troubled times. All he used to pay was a white goat or cock to the shrine master. That was then. In this modern age of ours we have got to pay more, more than we would love but it's got to be.

(He quickly pulls a pistol from his waist and bank notes from his jacket as he holds whisky bottle in the other hand. He raises both items, looking down as he stands in a commando style accompanied by hard drum beats in background. Enter Mura and Shapa, both visibly obsessed with the newspapers in their hands.)

MURA: Quite amazing! All this robbery went on behind our backs?

SHAPA: I tell you, our buddy Wenda is an old hand at every dirty trick. He convinced the deputy editor to allow this knock out publication.

(Throws fist in air.)

MURA: Is all this true? Where did the reporter get all this info?

SHAPA: Hey! Of course, I too have a hand in it. He verbally sacked me but now I've got him on the ropes. *(Clenches fist and almost jumps into the air.)* Justice never felt so good.

MURA: Watch out young man- if they get to know you and Wenda's role in this mess, you are surely going to pay dearly. This poses another court trial threat for the big men.

(He turns the newspaper pages.)

SHAPA: Nobody gonna know us. Cleverly masterminded by experts, man. They deserve it, they no gonna sit on top of us forever! Let dem feel the heat, dose of ya own medicine. *(Rasta accent.)*

MURA: They must now be sweating in hiding. A severe blow to their grand plans.

(Laughs as he exits.)

SHAPA: *(In Rasta voice and dance.)* Tell dem, ma people, nota joke wit jah man cauza you gotta be shut up. Tell dem, ma' all people, da' ya' man is too tough to sack, he gonna get you down da' drain.

SEE YA' ALL AT DA' CLUB TONITE.

WE GONNA CELEBRATE DE DRINK

GET OURSELVES CRAZY

DIS' NO MEAN SCORE

GOTTA A SPECIAL WAY

GONNA' COME ALONG

SEE U DE' MA' ALL PEOPLE.

(Repeat song to fade.)

(END OF ACT I.)

ACT II

SCENE 1

(Inside the large council hall, a little whispering, gossiping, laughing and loud page turning goes on. Suddenly, all members rise as the honorable speaker enters with her entourage to take the high table seats. Everybody keeps standing until the speaker is seated.)

ZAMWE: Ladies and gentlemen, welcome to this extraordinary meeting. It is necessary in the interest of saving and restoring our union's good image. We hope you have already read and understood the agenda, so, *(pauses)* we will now go straight to item number three in the interest of time.

KANGINE: Madam Speaker, there is no way we can jump items on the agenda before we adopt it, and not even a prayer to guide us? Imagine!

ZAMWE: Madam, with all due respect, there are a number of provisions in our constitution that guide such extraordinary sessions.

Prayer is not mandatory; it is just a conception of a believing heart.

KANGINE: Beginning on this note, I see no near end to the current troubles if we intend to counter darkness with more darkness. I thought prayer was a simple norm, which need not be complicated.

1ST FARMER: The issue of man praying for holy guidance and protection has been around since time immemorial. Why then sacrifice that divine right now?

BANDA: For heaven's sake, can we save time and focus on the real issues? Leave the spirits alone. None of your gods will plant maize for you.

2ND FARMER: We are propagating more dust as if we already don't have enough. Let us save the last unity drops left in shrewd hearts.

ZAMWE: *(Stern face.)* Order now? Welcome back from that break of emotional exchanges. I deliberately let it spark so as to prove the meaning of a crisis and extraordinary session. I'm neither a moral nor religious teacher, so let the legal side take control.

1ST FARMER: Madam Speaker, we are obliged to apply common sense in certain circumstances- but not interpret rules head on.

3RD FARMER: *(Fuming.)* To hell with your common sense. What use will it serve in the prevailing conditions?

ZAMWE: *(In a resigned manner.)* I think I'm losing control of the house, should we-

KONDO: Members! *(Bangs table.)* Can we exhibit maturity and respect for one another? Quite shameful to argue and counter argue as if in a bar!

(Silence resumes.)

ZAMWE: I have the ultimate mandate to run the affairs in this house. I'm legally empowered to evoke the rules against any disobeying member. Stop the nonsense now!

(She makes a serious face.)

SHAPA: Okay, on a sensible note now, can honorable speaker explain to us why she prematurely ended her official holiday? I thought we had a deputy speaker who could fulfill the role in her absence?

BANDA: Article fourteen-sub section two, part B talks of a speaker but not a deputy speaker, to preside over sessions.

2ND FARMER: Very vague reply, which insults our constitution! Anyway the question was directed to the speaker, thank you Mr. Know It All!

(Cheers and boos.)

ZAMWE: Members, *(pauses)* the gravity of the situation at hand, far more outweighs the luxurious holiday I was enjoying, moreover courtesy of your funds. It would be foolhardy of any responsible mind not to respond to such a call of a burning room at her own house. I hope I made no mistake in coming over?

(Big cheers and handclaps.)

MURA: That now leads us to the question of funds control. Whereas it is true that we agreed on the holiday-the expenditure was far above the usual.

BANDA: The unions' treasurer and president found it prudent. This was in appreciation of the diligent service she renders.

1ST FARMER: How can you exhaust the reserve funds in such a manner when we do not even have the season's fertilizers?

MURA: Even last year's debt owed to the marketing cooperative still stands!

1ST FARMER: From the financial report *(holds papers more closely)* I do not see the secretary's signature on the purported extra money paid out.

ZAMWE: Can the responsible people respond to those raised issues? As for me, I could not object an offer extended to me from your official democratically elected leaders.

KONDO: The issue of fertilizers has been put on hold as we are importing new, more modern ones this season, thus changing our usual suppliers. The same applies to the marketing cooperatives- we changed to professionals.

1ST FARMER: The present delays in procuring the said new modern fertilizers will deny us the opportunity of testing them.

KANGINE: We may end up losing a whole year's inputs if they are not sufficiently tested in the early rains.

MURA: How and why did you change the supplying and marketing groups without the whole board's consent?

KONDO: *(Wipes sweat off forehead.)* The new company supplying us is internationally recognized by many leading agricultural firms. Don't worry about the testing bit of it.

2ND FARMER: Mind you, the nature of soil varies from region to region. The wounds of the terrible losses four years back with those yellow substances are still fresh in our minds.

MURA: We are jumping a very important step here, we need to first know, why the change of suppliers and marketers, when they still did a good job?

ZAMWE: Surely, that should have been the first matter tackled. From the documents before me, I see that the meeting in which those decisions were passed, was fully attended by all concerned parties.

SHAPA: I do remember the meeting, but many objected to the idea of changing the suppliers and marketers before a performance verification report was made about them.

ZAMWE: But you did sign at the end of the minutes and meeting recommendations.

SHAPA: But, it is also clearly indicated in the minutes that I didn't subscribe to the idea of change. The signing was a mere confirmation of attendance.

MURA: The truth of the matter is that the issue was supposed to be on hold till further consultation. How it came to be passed, then, I don't know for sure!

3RD FARMER: Let the past be the past and concentrate on present issues-it seems some members' memories cannot serve them right.

1ST FARMER: That would be a grave mistake; few heads cannot compromise our future in the dirtiest of manners. That is why this meeting was called in the first place.

ZAMWE: Can I have the president iron out the confusion surrounding what was agreed upon in the said meeting?

KONDO: It is true that in the first committee meeting, we never reached common ground. However, this was eventually solved in the subsequent meetings.

MURA: Which meetings where these I never attended and no minutes were made?

KONDO: The person in charge of organizing such meetings and record keeping is just in front of you.

(Points to Shapa and a silence follows.)

SHAPA: Members, I feel it is time to clean out the closet. *(Pauses.)* The alleged subsequent meetings were actually ghost meetings. *(All faces turn.)* They were held in our president's living room over rounds of roasted meat and wine. *(The air becomes tense.)*

I was also invited as a special guest alongside your treasurer and another young lady I had never seen before.

MURA: Certainly, this serves as the root cause of the crisis if decisions are taken in bedrooms.

ZAMWE: Were these the same meetings where a decision to pay a law firm minus our legal consent was taken?

SHAPA: Not to my knowledge, Madam Speaker.

KANGINE: On that issue of legal costs, the case was against our president. At least, it would have been fair if he shared the costs with our treasury.

BANDA: The president was acting on the union's behalf as part of the campaign to lobby a seat on the national executive committee.

KANGINE: Does that give him a right to enter into crooked deals and forged cheques? One's lack of ethics and integrity need not be amended by the union coffers.

ZAMWE: Our legal team before other parties' act must first sanction issues on legal costs.

KONDO: *(Sensing danger.)* Ladies and gentlemen, I'm willing to act in the honorable manner expected of me. If thorough investigations are carried out to justify the present allegations, I will step down.

(A few handclaps.)

ZAMWE: Brilliant view from our president. It is in such moments that patriots are separated from politicians and men stand out from boys. *(Pauses. Silence.)* I'm also of the view that an independent commission of inquiry be formed in this case.

1ST FARMER: Good point, but let this commission be absolutely independent, free of the influence and communication from the union.

3RD FARMER: At least two or three members should be chosen amongst us to assist the commission in-

MURA: *(Serious.)* Not at all! A patient cannot be his or her own doctor. Absolute independence.

ZAMWE: Ok, enough. In my capacity, I now declare an independent commission of inquiry into the mismanagement and any scandals surrounding our farmers union.

2ND FARMER: What if we hired a leading law firm in town to sort us out?

KANGINE: We can as well involve the proven men of God from catch a fire church for more credibility.

ZAMWE: The composition of the commission is to be decided upon by our legal team and board of trustees. Meanwhile, all concerned parties should hand over their offices with immediate effect.

SHAPA: Madam Speaker, will the journalists be allowed to cover the proceedings of the commission of inquiry?

ZAMWE: Yes, of course, it will be open to the public. *(A few murmurs.)* Can someone lead us into the divine right of a closing prayer?

(She smiles.)

KANGINE: *(Standing with left hand raised.)* Let us pray. In the mighty name of the living God, I call for powerful divine judgment upon every soul before you, Lord. Let the unblemished be restored to glory and the wicked condemned to justice. Separate the sheep from goats and unleash the fire upon mortal man. Dear God, let the wailing of your children be heard. Amen.

ZAMWE: Our legal advisor's office remains open for any updates and inquiries. Go in peace.

(Members stand up, some stretching, yawning, whispering in groups, and the speaker's entourage exits first.)

(End of Scene 1 of Act II. Lights change.)

SCENE 2

(Inside a modern bar, in a half lit corner, bottles, glasses and files are on the round glass table. Two men sit. Kondo talks on his mobile phone, as Banda turns a newspaper page. Slow music can be heard in background.)

KONDO: We need to be on guard on all frontiers, you never know from which side they will hit us hardest. Get everybody ready.

(Hangs up.)

BANDA: I'm still perturbed by that lady speaker's conduct of the session. We were never going to get that far, if she had followed our instructions.

KONDO: Damned woman! Did no good. She just let the bastards push me to the wall.

BANDA: I expected her to turn the wave anytime and kill off the bloody arguments. Was surprised to hear her second a commission of inquiry.

KONDO: The pressure was really too much for me. Had to free myself a bit, thus the proposal. Anyway, past is past. We now focus on how to shut up the new openings.

(Two skimpily dressed ladies enter and the two men simultaneously turn to gaze at them till they disappear around a corner.)

BANDA: Should first get clues on which people to form that commission of inquiry. Our immediate source, Zamwe, looks to be off the hook.

KONDO: I'm still a bit hopeful that Zamwe can still help in a way. The session decisions she took were unavoidable given the firing squads of the opposition.

BANDA: Why not give her a call to come over now? We can start on a high with her.

KONDO: Pray that her new husband has not returned.

(Picks phone, dials a number and puts on ear.)

BANDA: Didn't she sack that one too before the holiday – she is now searching.

(He laughs.)

KONDO: Sorry for her. *(He signals for Banda to shut up.)* Hello Madam. I'm of the view that you join me and our treasurer at Hotel Vibrations so as to sort you out of the holiday financial mess. Make sure you are not seen, use the side entrance. Quick, ok. *(Puts phone down.)* She is coming.

BANDA: We should order that tough whisky to knock her out of her rigidity. As soon she comes, the hot topics begin too. No time to waste.

KONDO: No need of pressurizing her. She needs to feel warm and friendly, then, the hot topics creep in slowly.

(Empties his glass.) Past experiences have taught me not to live a one-way traffic business life.

BANDA: Sure, we need an alternative to fall back to in case the present ventures fail.

KONDO: I already have an alternative. Maybe it's time to let you to know, and perhaps join us.

BANDA: *(Visibly impressed.)* Is it beginning soon? Tell me.

KONDO: Well, while I was abroad last year, I met this former colleague, now in exile. We are to run two farming businesses in the North of this country.

BANDA: That calls for big land, an essential factor in such business.

KONDO: Currently, land is in plenty in the Northern region. Due to a prolonged rebellion there, many natives left their homes or were killed altogether, leaving behind vast areas of land that lie idle.

BANDA: But, how can you survive in such an insecure area?

KONDO: *(Sips from glass.)* Well, brains and tongues play key roles here. My friend in exile has good connections with the rebels and I'm to ally with our government too in similar manner.

BANDA: *(Worriedly.)* So, you are to supply both sides with arms and ammunition.

KONDO: Not that. I told you, we are to do extensive farming, supply either side with food and sell off the surplus and of course we also target the golden drugs that can make one a billionaire in an instant.

BANDA: But the north is largely dry, there is no ideal climate for farming.

KONDO: We are to do business along the ever flowing River Nile.

BANDA: How about source of labour if there are no people in homes?

KONDO: Our firm on the government side will use labour from refugee camps whereas the partner firm on the rebel wing will draw its labour from abductees and rebel ranks themselves. Quite cheap, as you only pay the commanders some cigar packs.

BANDA: But, insecurity still reigns and if you are discovered of double dealing on either side... *(pauses)* problems?

KONDO: Listen, *(pauses)* I've only told you in this country, no other person knows it here. I'm to apply for land like any other investor. Nobody in this country apart from you knows of the other side of the story.

BANDA: You can trust me to keep the word to myself. Always a gentleman.

KONDO: My friend in exile has already started with his part on the rebel wing, I'm only being delayed by the tender board bosses in our army here.

BANDA: What kind of food do you intend to supply?

KONDO: We are growing the usual food crops and then keeping some cows, goats and poultry.

BANDA: How about garden drugs?

KONDO: You cannot obviously mention such in a business proposal, that's mafia business that is internationally acknowledged.

BANDA: Do you think the government will give you a go ahead in that region?

KONDO: I'm first getting it in the right channels, and if they fail, I resort to the side ways, but it has got to be done.

BANDA: Like you said, one cannot put all his eggs in one basket. Munga Farmers Union is crumbling any day now.

KONDO: Precisely. Many guys are reaping fortunes from this northern conflict. That's the reason it is not ending soon.

BANDA: I have also heard of such merry-war stories.

KONDO: In fact, if all goes well, this might be a grand business deal to be reckoned with, but of course highly secretive.

BANDA: It needs first class intelligence and consciousness.

KONDO: We have plans of trading combatant intelligence information to either side depending on the situation.

BANDA: That means you have to get close to the top chief spies of either side.

KONDO: That's our aim. There you are guaranteed full time protection, red passport and money with no accountability.

BANDA: You became a king on your own, out of symbiosis.

KONDO: That's the way, and I can assure you that we are not the first in this business. It has been around since time immemorial.

BANDA: I remember reading of such in one high school novel.

KONDO: There are big governments and leading business people from western countries making it a habit especially in African war zones.

BANDA: That's the reason why Africa is never short of wars.

KONDO: I tell you, no opportunity is put to waste by sharp eagle-eyed guys.

BANDA: *(Laughing.)* These days, people even make profits from funerals.

KONDO: Others go ahead to fake deaths and funerals in the name of making quick money.

(He laughs.)

BANDA: It is said that a cow's tears is the dog's happiness.

KONDO: Tit for tat, survival of the fittest.

BANDA: Every man for himself. (*Toasts glasses, cheers, and big laughter.*) Some roasted meat too; drinks on an empty stomach are really dangerous. I guess three plates are enough.

(Rushes off to the counter.)

(End of Scene 2 of Act II.)

SCENE 3

(Meanwhile the two skimpily dressed ladies return, one waves to lonely Kondo. They proceed to a dimly lit opposite corner near the entrance where they engage in an inciting dance to reveal their naked body parts. A few revelers join and take some wine bottles to them as gifts. Suddenly, the two ladies storm off the floor giggling seductively and exit. Kondo recollects himself as Banda returns)

KONDO: The young funny girls did their best to engage us in their business for a while.

BANDA: I was about to join them before they stormed out, the music was not bad either.

KONDO: They are hired by hotel managers to entertain the likes of you.

(Zamwe enters from a small door on the side, dressed in blue jean trousers, matching jean jacket and red top.)

ZAMWE: Was lonely and stressed at home. My kids are still on the trip and so I decided to pass time with you guys.

KONDO: *(Gesturing to the empty chair.)* Still feeling the luxurious holiday hung over? What was it like in the Caribbean?

ZAMWE: *(Removes jacket to reveal tight top.)* Plenty of swimming, sunbathing, volleyball and drinking.

(Laughs as she pours whisky into her glass.)

BANDA: Your new cut figure says it all. Did all those activities, while half naked, in the so-called swimsuits!

(Laughs.)

ZAMWE: *(Smiling.)* It is the order of the day. You know-people those ends do not shun nakedness like we do here.

KONDO: Sorry for rushing you back but it was worth it. We plan to reward you more of that if the current storms stabilize.

BANDA: This time it may be to a place where people go completely naked along beaches.

(Laughs and falls back in chair.)

ZAMWE: *(Smiling.)* Perhaps, you know of such a place and have been there too.

(Downs glass and pours more.)

BANDA: My faith does not allow such...

ZAMWE: Eeh... you too have a religion!

(She laughs harder. Meanwhile Kondo is visibly obsessed with something in the far corner.)

KONDO: Someone keeps beckoning me from the other side.

BANDA: Maybe some thug wants your wallet.

KONDO: Looks like a lady I know.

(A lady in a long dress and high-heeled shoes comes over to Kondo's side, presses her hand on his shoulder, smiles and murmurs some greetings to the other two. She bends and whispers to Kondo and immediately the two move together to the other side.) Little business here, back soon.

(He stands up and follows the lady.)

ZAMWE: Is this lady your colleague?

BANDA: Yes, but she came late for her appointment.

ZAMWE: Why does she fear us?

BANDA: I think she is new to the country, so not yet used to the natives.

ZAMWE: The liquor is really tough, better get home early and relax before I stagger from here.

BANDA: Don't mind, just eat more meat and the liquor gets absorbed. *(Pours more into her glass.)* One needs such to forget the bad times we have had.

ZAMWE: What kind of sorting did you call me up for? I thought the holiday package was legal?

BANDA: Yes, but you know how our enemies can come up with anything to tarnish our names. We need to be on guard.

ZAMWE: *(Shouting.)* Who are those and what can they do?

BANDA: You know, we have bad characters in our union. They go on implicating you and us in all sorts of silly deals that hide the good in us.

ZAMWE: No! No! *(Slaps table.)* This cannot go on like this. It will surely kill off the whole union.

BANDA: Slow down a bit. We better wait for Mr. President before we plunge too deep into murky waters of the union.

(In the far corner, Kondo and his lady kiss each other passionately, while Banda and Zamwe look on in disbelief.)

ZAMWE: Is this all I came to witness? God save us!

BANDA: Quite unbelievable, why couldn't they move upstairs? Chasing the wrong business.

ZAMWE: *(Slurring her words.)* My time is up, let me go to sleep.

(Rises up, but staggers and holds on to chair.)

BANDA: Hold on my dear, wait for the body to get strong.

ZAMWE: Foolish, do you know my strength, go and drown. I've got to go!

(She takes two steps, staggers and falls flat on floor. Banda shouts as he jumps to rescue her. Kondo comes rushing over with his shirt unbuttoned halfway.)

KONDO: What is the problem?

BANDA: She just had too much of it and cannot support herself. *(Shouting as a waiter rushes in with a glass of water.)* Bring some cold water!

KONDO: She needs a little bit of relaxation. Get her upstairs to the room before driving her home. I'm collecting more water.

(*Meanwhile, the lady who was kissing Kondo stealthily goes to their table, picks a mobile phone and some money from a bag before exiting quickly.*)

BANDA: Get all the bills cleared, not forgetting our documents on the table. You brought the delay- we would have left by now!

(*He holds Zamwe by the waist as the two slowly move upstairs. Kondo stands on the counter paying the bills to the playing background tune of "It is not easy".*)

(END OF ACT II.)

ACT III

SCENE 1

(On a narrow village path surrounded by low bushes, Mura and Kangine move along, insects and birds sing in the evening hours. Kangine is in a long dress with a head turban. Mura is in gumboots, brown trousers and a gray t-shirt.)

MURA: The wife told me yesterday that he had a slight headache and had begun eating well. She had gone to collect the last drug dose.

KANGINE: These days, medicine alone is not enough. One needs spiritual food too.

MURA: Could be some resurgent malaria, though Shapa said malaria is never among his sicknesses.

KANGINE: That young man needs proper guidance otherwise, he might ruin himself.

MURA: No sound of music from his house. He must really be sick.

(They turn a small bend around a fence and are soon in Shapa's compound. Shapa is seated in a shade on the right hand corner. He smiles and welcomes his guests to take seats.)

SHAPA: I'm now better than I was yesterday. Preparing to face the commission of inquiry anytime.

MURA: Maybe the commission has something to do with that prolonged sickness? You know the fear, stress and thoughts that come up.

(He smiles a bit.)

KANGINE: Thank God you are now better. I was worried when Mura told me of your sickness. I left the farm and came praying all the way that we find you improved.

SHAPA: As a man, I have to lift myself up because the family was getting worried with each passing hour. Wenda too called this afternoon saying that things looked bright on my official side.

MURA: You mean the union stuff?

SHAPA: Yes, certainly that. He added that I was born lucky but did not elaborate. I'm relieved and anxious to hear more.

KANGINE: My prayers and catch a fire miracles slowly enfolding for mankind. More manifestation to come, God has promised us.

MURA: *(Smiling.)* I remember your prayer for everybody to catch a fire. It has now begun with Shapa, if his words are to be counted on.

(Laughs.)

SHAPA: Next it's you, my man.

(Laughs too.)

KANGINE: God's power comes in its own timing and will. Man has no control over it or its direction.

MURA: *(Smiling.)* Happy are those who believe without seeing. You are not sick *(points to Shapa)* but just experiencing a holy fire. Amen.

SHAPA: Hope it is true, my Lord. Amen.

(Both men laugh.)

KANGINE: *(Composed.)* In whatever we do, plan or think, God has the ultimate say. I invite all of you, your friends and families to a special healing service come this Sunday at our church.

MURA: Maybe you can organize for a special Munga farmers healing crusade, as well.

KANGINE: No need for those divisions. We have one God and one human race. Munga farmers are not special.

Catch a fire is not discriminatory, just like a family cock which crows for the whole village. *(Looks at watch.)* I have got to join my prayer warriors. Be blessed.

(Exits.)

SHAPA: *(Shouting after her.)* Pray that the fire does not finish us up. The prophetess is gone. We can now enjoy the true taste.

(Shapa dashes into a room and returns carrying a pot with three long straws inside. He places it in the middle and the two first make a high five before suckling.)

MURA: You have killed my evening farm work now. Hope I find my tools safe tomorrow in the field where I left them.

SHAPA: Why didn't you drop them at your store?

MURA: I thought I would return quickly as lady Kangine too said she would make a quick visit.

SHAPA: The planting has to wait till the commission solves the issue.

MURA: Anyway, that's it; let the true taste of our land reign.

(Bends and drinks. Wenda enters the scene.)

SHAPA: Hey! *(Stands up.)* Here comes the lost sheep Mr. Reporter. You have lost weight, what's up?

WENDA: Been busy building the nation in a professional manner. (*Laughs and continues to shake hands with the two men.*) Got tired of you people's underhanded wrangles.

(Quickly grabs one of the straws before even taking a seat.)

MURA: After fueling the conflict, you sit on the fence and look blameless.

WENDA: *(Taking a seat.)* This drink is classic. I only get to taste it when I visit you- village people.

SHAPA: You live by a forced fasting, sorry boy, the town stuff is too expensive for the likes of you.

(Laughs.)

WENDA: *(Rising from the pot.)* The big news! *(Pauses.)* Could anybody apart from us be listening? *(All turn to look around.)* The trees and walls have ears these days. The papers tomorrow will bomb us with exclusive behind-the-scenes news of the big fish in the dirtiest of waters.

MURA: Yet another scandal!

(His eyes open wide.)

SHAPA: Am I implicated in it too? *(Worriedly.)*

WENDA: The mother of all scandals, but this time, the small men are safe. *(Pats Shapa on the shoulder.)* The three executives drank themselves into ruin and everlasting shame.

SHAPA: Sure?

(Half standing as Wenda takes a deep sip.)

MURA: Could the third executive be our honorable speaker?

WENDA: That's right, but I'm supposed to let the details bomb you through the press tomorrow, you know, professional ethics.

(Smiles and sips more.)

SHAPA: Man! *(Squats in front of Wenda.)* Be a gent, we too are gentlemen, and you know our past deals, let the cat out, man!

WENDA: Ok, they eventually ended up raping in addition to flirting with some ladies of the night. Total mess, I tell you.

(Drinks more.)

MURA: I suppose all this went on at night?

WENDA: Surely. Drank themselves silly, fought each other and all the foolishness that comes with it real or imaginary.

SHAPA: Where was this?

WENDA: Hotel Vibrations, in the ultra-modern executive wing. Lady Zamwe got too drunk to help herself and the lions took advantage.

MURA: How come they were only three?

WENDA: Sources say it all started as a meeting, which culminated into a drinking spree.

SHAPA: And they can't pull moneybags out, to stop you people from publishing such a scandal?

WENDA: They made that attempt, at first, with the hotel workers, but gossip is gossip. Only one senior editor has been standing in our way pending further investigations.

MURA: That editor might have swallowed much tea to kill off the story.

WENDA: Maybe, but he now seems to have removed the embargo. It is a green light now.

SHAPA: Shock waves await the whole nation. Poor Zamwe, caught up in the den!

MURA: Then the police again pick up from there and court proceedings resume.

SHAPA: That surely condemns Munga Farmers Union to everlasting death.

WENDA: Possibly, you get to survive the would-have-been cumbersome commission of inquiry.

(Smiling.)

MURA: Justice never rots. One day, we have to return to our own.

SHAPA: I feel sorry for their families. The weight of all this upon them. Kangine's fire, perhaps, spreading too far.

MURA: Double tragedy, but we have got to pick ourselves up quickly and rock the ship forward. The captain is not recovering soon.

(Takes a deep sip.)

SHAPA: I would love to celebrate this second knock out but should first confirm with the press tomorrow.

WENDA: *(Rising from the seat, shouting.)* Stop worrying, guys, this is our time while we still live. You never know what tomorrow holds. This is life, men! *(Louder.)* Get up, style up.

(Stands up and jigs to his rap. Shapa joins Wenda in the jig, arms in air while Mura plays the straws around the pot to make accompanying beats.)

CHORUS:

DIS NO FIRST NO LAST

GOTTA FEEL IN GOTTA TASTE IT

WHILE YOU BREATHS

IT GONNA DRY UP

FEEL- IN SORRY, OR BOY

FEEL- IN GREAT OR MAN

FEEL- IN THE FIRE

FEEL- IN THE VIBRATIONS

(Shapa and Wenda spice up the fray with coordinated dance strokes. Mura increases the rhythm from the pot and chairs around him.)

(End of Scene 1 of Act III.)

FINAL SCENE

(In a small compound with a grass-thatched hut in the middle, hoes, pangas and baskets lean on the mud wall. Three men sit in a semi-circle. Two with folded arms on their laps and the other with one hand stroking his chin.)

1ST FARMER: I could see trouble boiling up but this really goes to the extreme.

2ND FARMER: Why did Banda shoot poor Shapa yet it was he alone in the mess?

1ST FARMER: They always suspected young Shapa of sabotage and linking their secrets to the press.

2ND FARMER: Pray that they survive the serious injuries and live to face justice.

3RD FARMER: *(Waking up.)* Are they still alive?

2ND FARMER: Yes, police shot Banda in the leg as he tried to escape after injuring Shapa on the shoulder. It is said Banda was acting on Kondo's orders, the owner of the pistol.

1ST FARMER: The next victim was to be the newspaper editor. He in turn sacked journeyman Wenda for allegedly taking bribes and collaborating with the monsters.

3RD FARMER: That journalist was a chameleon. He ate from all angles, even masterminded the bloody publications that ignited the fire.

2ND FARMER: At first I didn't believe the allegations, but now that a lot of vengeance and revenge has gone on, it is true that the rape did occur.

1ST FARMER: Lady Zamwe is one big disgrace, with all the due respect she commanded. The legal fraternity must disband her.

2ND FARMER: She too lies in hospital for trauma now, alongside the scandalous masters.

1ST FARMER: I'm sure Banda is joining Kondo in the cooler as soon as his health improves.

3RD FARMER: *(Fuming.)* You people never liked our bosses and you contributed to their downfall.

(Spits.)

1ST FARMER: *(Equally furious.)* Foolish! Were any of us buying them the liquor or funding their dubious deals?

2ND FARMER: In fact it is you *(points to 3rd farmer)* who always networked with those thieving bandits. We knew you all along as their spy and you got paid for that cheap role! Shame on you.

(He laughs.)

3RD FARMER: *(Standing up.)* Bastards! Does that call for your bloody talk and rejoicing? Who was not benefiting from the union? You bought shares, I didn't.

(Kicks one of them. They all rise and chase him, one falls down and 3rd farmer disappears off stage.)

2ND FARMER: The fool, he too deserves the comfort of the cells or hospital bed.

(Dusts off his trousers.)

1ST FARMER: *(Returning.)* The bastard survives to die another day. Opening a snake's mouth to look at its teeth!

2ND FARMER: What worries me more, is the money our union owes me. I'm destined for a dark end.

1ST FARMER: Some of us got loans that may now end up taxing us more interest than we would have desired.

2ND FARMER: Or get lucky when the union collapses and we walk off freely.

1ST FARMER: Oh no! There has to be a debt and assets recovery tribunal by the board of trustees.

2ND FARMER: *(Picking up his hoe and panga.)* I'm off to the bar till morning.

(Walks off slowly with hoe on shoulder.)

1ST FARMER: *(Calling after him.)* Maybe, we try out Kangine's fire band performing tonight at the playground.

(Sits and places chin on hand, as a mellow song plays in background till fade. End of play.)

(END OF PLAY. CURTAINS ARE DRAWN.)

To read other works by KHAMEL Publishing, please visit:

www.khamelpublishing.com